STYRACOSAURUS

AND OTHER LAST DINOSAURS

by **Dougal Dixon**

illustrated by
Steve Weston and **James Field**

PiCTURE WiNDOW BOOKS
Minneapolis, Minnesota

Picture Window Books
5115 Excelsior Boulevard
Suite 232
Minneapolis, MN 55416
877-845-8392
www.picturewindowbooks.com

Printed in the United States of America.

Library of Congress Cataloging-in-Publication Data
Dixon, Dougal.
Styracosaurus and other last dinosaurs / by Dougal
Dixon ; illustrated by Steve Weston & James Field.
p. cm. – (Dinosaur find)
Includes bibliographical references and index.
ISBN 1-4048-1329-2 (hard cover)
1. Dinosaurs-—Extinction—Juvenile literature.
2. Styracosaurus-—Juvenile literature. I. Weston, Steve,
ill. II. Field, James, 1959- ill. III. Title.
QE861.6.E95D59 2006
567.9-—dc22   2005023145

Acknowledgments
This book was produced for Picture Window Books
by Bender Richardson White, U.K.

Illustrations by James Field (pages 4–5, 7, 15, 17,21)
and Steve Weston (cover and pages 9, 11, 13, 19).
Diagrams by Stefan Chabluk.
All photographs copyright Digital Vision except
page 14 (John Zimmermann/Frank Lane Picture
Agency).

Consultant: John Stidworthy, Scientific Fellow of
the Zoological Society, London, and former
Lecturer in the Education Department, Natural
History Museum, London.

Reading Adviser: Susan Kesselring, M.A., Literacy
Educator, Rosemount-Apple Valley-Eagan
(Minnesota) School District

Types of dinosaurs

In this book, a red shape at the top of a left-hand page shows the animal was a meat-eater. A green shape shows it was a plant-eater.

Just how big—or small— were they?

Dinosaurs were many different sizes. We have compared their sizes to one of the following:

Chicken
2 feet (60 centimeters) tall
6 pounds (2.7 kilograms)

Adult person
6 feet (1.8 meters) tall
170 pounds (76.5 kg)

Elephant
10 feet (3 m) tall
12,000 pounds
(5,400 kg)

TABLE OF CONTENTS

WHAT'S INSIDE?

Dinosaurs lived between 230 and 65 million years ago. These dinosaurs were some of the last. Find out how they lived and what they have in common with today's animals.

THE LAST DINOSAURS

At the very end of the Age of Dinosaurs, there were some of the most spectacular dinosaurs that ever lived—duckbilled plant-eaters, armored plant-eaters, horned plant-eaters, and huge meat-eaters.

A herd of *Anatotitan* ate at the edge of a forest. A horned *Triceratops* finished drinking at the river. A fierce *Albertosaurus* eyed them hungrily from the shadows.

5

ALBERTOSAURUS

Pronunciation:
al-BURR-toe-SAW-rus

One of the biggest and last of the meat-eating dinosaurs was *Albertosaurus*. It prowled through the forests, looking for other animals to hunt. With its sharp teeth, it could saw meat and crush bone.

Bone-crusher today

Leopards use their strong jaws and teeth to crush bone like *Albertosaurus* did millions of years ago.

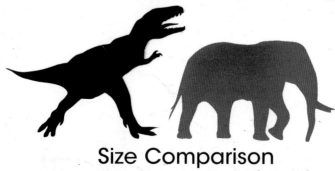

Size Comparison

Albertosaurus usually hunted its own food. If it saw an animal that was already dead, it would eat that instead of hunting.

STEGOCERAS

Pronunciation:
ste-GOS-uh-rus

Stegoceras had a lump of bone on the top of its head. It probably used this lump as a battering ram or for showing off to other dinosaurs. Most of the time, *Stegoceras* was a gentle plant-eater.

Bony head today

The African buffalo has big horns that make it look big and fierce like *Stegoceras* looked with its bony lump.

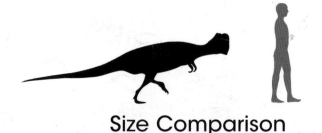

Size Comparison

Stegoceras could run quickly on its hind legs. Whenever danger threatened, it ran off and hid among plants. The bone-headed dinosaurs were among the last to appear.

STYRACOSAURUS

Pronunciation:
sty-RACK-o-SAW-rus

Styracosaurus had an enormous horn on its nose. It also had a row of big horns all around its neck shield. Anything attacking a *Styracosaurus* would have been quite scared.

Looking fierce today

An angry African elephant makes itself look fearsome and charges with its head down like *Styracosaurus* did.

Size Comparison

When a *Styracosaurus* was threatened, it would turn to face its attacker. Its horns and neck shield made *Styracosaurus* look bigger and fiercer than it really was.

PANOPLOSAURUS

Pronunciation:
PAN-oh-pluh-SAW-rus

Panoplosaurus was an armored dinosaur. It had huge spikes sticking out of its sides and shoulders. It used its armor to keep away meat-eaters and to fight other *Panoplosaurus*.

Fighting today

Rhinoceroses lock their horns and push each other when they are fighting like *Panoplosaurus* did years ago.

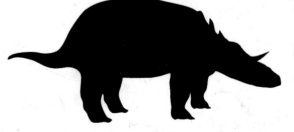

Size Comparison

When two *Panoplosaurus* fought one another to lead the herd, they locked their spikes together and pushed. The strongest dinosaur pushed the other away and became the leader.

PARASAUROLOPHUS

Pronunciation:
PAR-uh-SAW-ro-LOH-fus

Parasaurolophus had a long crest sweeping back from the top of its head. It could snort through this and make a noise like a musical instrument. *Parasaurolophus* talked to other animals in its herd by snorting.

Forest talk today

Like *Parasaurolophus*, Okapis have good hearing and listen for one another in thick forests.

Size Comparison

Parasaurolophus had a ducklike beak. It's often called a duckbill dinosaur. The beak was used to help it pluck leaves from trees.

EUOPLOCEPHALUS

One of the last of the armored dinosaurs was *Euoplocephalus*. Its head, back, and tail were covered in armored plates. There was a bony lump on the end of its tail that it used as a club.

On the defense today

Hippopotamuses are mostly peaceful animals but will defend themselves when threatened like *Euoplocephalus* did.

Size Comparison

Euoplocephalus kept away from other kinds of animals. It stayed close to other *Euoplocephalus* without fighting.

LEPTOCERATOPS

Pronunciation:
LEP-tuh-SER-uh-tops

Leptoceratops was a horned dinosaur about the size of a pig. It had a narrow skull and a big beak like a parrot. It probably walked on four legs and could run fast. *Leptoceratops* was one of the last of the dinosaurs.

Small plant-eater today

Prairie dogs are tiny animals that nibble, chop, snip, and grind food like *Leptoceratops* did long ago.

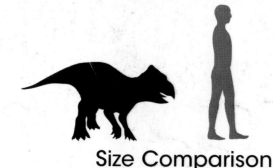

Size Comparison

Leptoceratops ate plants close to the ground. The color and markings of its skin may have helped it hide from its predators.

19

TRICERATOPS

Pronunciation:
tri-SAIR-uh-tops

At the very end of the Age of Dinosaurs came *Triceratops*. With its big head and three horns, it would have frightened off most attackers. It used its big beak to feed on tough plants.

Weapons today

Like the *Triceratops*, the warthog uses the weapons on its big head to keep enemies away.

Size Comparison

20

Triceratops was always on the move, looking for plants to eat and meat-eating dinosaurs to avoid.

21

WHERE DID THEY GO?

Dinosaurs are extinct, which means that none of them are alive today. Scientists study rocks and fossils to find clues about what happened to dinosaurs.

People have different explanations about what happened. Some people think a huge asteroid hit Earth and caused all sorts of climate changes, which caused the dinosaurs to die. Others think volcanic eruptions caused the climate to change and that killed the dinosaurs. No one knows for sure what happened to all the dinosaurs.

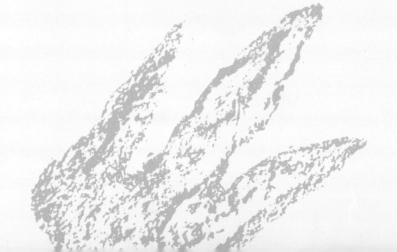

GLOSSARY

armor—protective covering of plates, horns, spikes, or clubs used for fighting

beak—the hard front part of the mouth of birds and some dinosaurs

crest—structure on top of the head or along the back, usually used to signal to other animals

herds—large groups of animals that move, feed, and sleep together

horns—pointed structures on the head

prowl—to move slowly and silently

shield—a piece of armor

To Learn More

At the Library

Clark, Neil, and William Lindsay. *1001 Facts About Dinosaurs.* New York: Backpack Books, Dorling Kindersley, 2002.

Dixon, Dougal. *Dougal Dixon's Amazing Dinosaurs.* Honesdale, Penn.: Boyds Mills Press, 2000.

Holtz, Thomas, and Michael Brett-Surman. *Jurassic Park Institute Dinosaur Field Guide.* New York: Random House, 2001.

On the Web

FactHound offers a safe, fun way to find Web sites related to this book. All of the sites on FactHound have been researched by our staff.

1. Visit *www.facthound.com*
2. Type in this special code: 1404813292
3. Click on the FETCH IT button.

Your trusty FactHound will fetch the best sites for you!

Look for all of the books in the Dinosaur Find series:

Index